# Along the Way

## Observations, Thoughts,
## and Portraits in Rhyme and Meter

### Poetry by Tova S. Milinsky

WISDOM PRESS

**Along the Way**
Observations, Thoughts,
and Portraits in Rhyme and Meter

Copyright © 2014 by Tova S. Milinsky
Layout and cover design by Jacqueline L. Challiss Hill
Cover Photo by Ariel Milinsky
Printed in the United States of America

Summary: A collection of poems by Tova S. Milinsky.

Library of Congress Cataloging-in-Publication Data
    Milinsky, Tova S.
    Along the Way/Tova S. Milinsky–First Edition
    ISBN-13: 978-1-938326-36-3
    1. Poetry. 2. Literary collections.
    I. Milinsky, Tova S. II. Title
    Library of Congress Control Number: 2014943601

WISDOM PRESS

Wisdom Press is an imprint of Nelson Publishing & Marketing
366 Welch Road, Northville, MI 48167
www.nelsonpublishingandmarketing.com
(248) 735-0418

# Contents

# Life Along the Way

# Portraits

# Changing Times: Penetrating the Imponderable

# The New Way: The Future

* "The Call of Rusty Rustle" and "Snowtime" were originally published in *Coming and Goings*, (Ferne Press, 2013). Permission to reprint granted by Ferne Press.

# Acknowledgments

First and foremost, I must acknowledge the support and guidance of my editors, Wisdom Press (a division of Nelson Publishing & Marketing), and my liaison therein, Marian Nelson, as well as my daughter, Beth Hedva, Ph.D., without whom the book would not have reached completion.

Appreciation must also be given to indefatigable Kris Yankee, who is the editor and project manager of Wisdom Press. A sincere and grateful thank you goes to my dearest longtime friend, Mania Salinger, herself the author of her own edifying memoir, *Looking Back,* who referred me to Marian Nelson in the first place.

Also, many thanks to my family and children: Debby Milinsky and Assad Sobky; Sharon Milinsky and Jeffrey Axelrod, and Joel and Yvonne Milinsky; and Harold Finkleman, all of whom contributed support and love throughout the project. I also want to include my five grandchildren, Vanessa Nizic, Travis Wright, Jamie and Sara Axelrod, and Ariel Milinsky, for all their wonderful love and support.

# Foreword

By Marilyn McGrath, Writing Teacher and Author of *All You Know on Earth*

I have been writing alongside Tova Milinsky since 1999. That is a long time. I have seen the way her quiet frustration explodes into joy when, at last, her vision finds words and her words fit the form. I have watched a roomful of writers look up, smiling, knowing she will share her discovery with them. Yes, some of these poems did emerge from assignments I have in class, but most developed later, in solitude, as good writing surely must. These poems began with the breath of an idea, an inspiration, and were coaxed into being by the poet's patience and hard work.

Tova has a keen ear for classical meter and rhyme scheme like the pantoum, villanelle, and medieval French rondeau. She is so skilled in these forms, so nimble, and even playful at times, that readers might actually think it an easy thing to do. My suggestion: look up just one of these poetic terms and then try to write a poem following the specific pattern. I dare you. But there is so much more to her work than merely finding the right rhythm and rhyme.

As she says, "poetry is more than verbal play." First and foremost, it is Tova's great heart that creates her poems; her wit merely gives them shape.

As a poet and human being, she is intrigued by the many challenges life presents, not the least of which is growing older. And her honesty can be disarming, as when she writes about the unwelcome intrusion of forgetfulness: "Words in hiding as I age / Set new limits on the page." Never maudlin, Tova simply gives a nod to this annoyance and moves on. Another major challenge she recognizes is the profound and confounding inability for one person to ever know what is inside another's heart or soul. Whether it is the woman in "Legacy" who carries her sister-in-law's unborn child for her after her own sons are killed in an automobile crash or the enigmatic farmer making plans in "Field of Dreams," there is a prevailing sense that some dreams can never be shared and most people's motives remain a mystery no matter what we think we know. If this is not a clarion call for us to be less judgmental, I don't know what is.

The poems in this collection, varied as they are, reflect the poet's sincere hope that people everywhere will one day sit up and pay attention, will be curious and forgiving, and will take a stand to live deeply and wisely "within the truth of tempered thought." In her personal life, as well as her poems, Tova embodies both the head and heart, both sense and sensibility. It has been my honor, my pleasure, and my joy to sit beside her at the table all these years and write.

# Author's Note and Introduction

Because my first poetry book was *Comings and Goings*, it felt natural to me that this one should be called *Along the Way*. It is a continuation of "the road." *Along the Way* has four sections representing a continuation of the road we travel in life.

I wanted the first section to be humorous, whimsical, yet reflective of life along the way, hence its title, "Life Along the Way."

The next section, "Portraits," was very important to me as a composite of stories in poetic form that describe who we are.

"Changing Times," the third section, is an example of our interaction with the rapid reorientation of our social relationships.

The final section, "The New Way," expresses our observations, hopes, and ambivalence about what is yet to come.

It is my fondest hope that the book will find sensitive souls who will delight in being witness to a new beginning.

# Preface

*The essence of a poem, for me, is depth of thought and feeling. Some poems may be succinct, while others may ramble. Many rhymes may be written, but not all qualify. It is to this "quest" to write poetry that expresses depth of thought and feeling that my Rondeau (and this book of poems) refers.*

*Now my poem:*

# Rondeau[1]

---

[1] The rondeau is written on two rhymes throughout: thirteen full-length lines and two briefer unrhymed refrains. The refrain may consist of the first half of the first line but may consist merely of the first word. The fifteen lines are grouped in three stanzas, the first of five lines, the second of three lines and refrain, and the third of five lines and refrain. According to the *Complete Rhyming Dictionary*, edited by Clement Wood, (Cleveland, 1933), 50, "The Rondeau, . . . is a fifteen-line poem of eight or ten syllable lines. It is divided into three stanzas of unequal length, knit together by two rhymed sounds and a refrain taken out of the first line. . . .The rhyme scheme is:
one, one, two, two, one;
one, one, two, R;
one, one, two, two, one, R."

To write a poem in a special way
To ponder on each word or rhythm's lay
While searching for the phrase that says it best
As exercise, or lark, or ego's test,

The challenge lies in will the words convey
The message of my heart or, will they say
I play a game; but, I may learn someday
(if I continue faithful to my quest)
To write a poem.

For poetry is more than verbal play
Which shallow sentiments can well gainsay
While heart and beauty intertwined attest
That these components hold one's interest
Thus even novices might then essay
To write a poem.

# Life Along the Way

## Hello, Millennium

Look back when we were very young,
A sheltered life we led.
The good was right, the bad was wrong,
Our dreams still lay ahead.

We knew the path that we would take,
There was an ordered plan.
The road to womanhood lay left.
Lay right, were you a man.

The road was very simple then,
The choices all too few.
Men worked to earn a living wage
And knew what they could do.

Then all at once our lives were changed
We called it progress then.
The world grew smaller all at once
We hardly knew just when.

Today we know too much too soon.
Our options are unbound.
And far from bringing happiness,
There's chaos all around.

No doubt the pendulum will swing,
We'll blend with the New Age.
We're so much wiser now, you know,
It's time to turn the page.

## Creativity

Some poems come unbidden
They just appear and stay
Their ending may be hidden
But they brook no delay

They're varied in their substance
Their urgency is great
Just what they're representing
Is not supposed to wait

A stanza in the present
A rhythm from within
Reminding me they're still around
And keeps me in a spin

I'd master this dilemma
That conceals what I should learn
If I figured out what's not revealed
And got the wheels to turn

So cancel all appointments
And let the light shine in
I'm ripe for revelation
Inspiration can begin

## Never Say Never

"Beard the lion in his den"
That is what I'm doing when
I attempt to write again
Poetry with meter

"What?" you say, "What is the trick?"
"What makes you think the words won't click?"
Lines with rhyme and rhythm "tick"
In Poetry with meter

Years ago the words appeared
Tripping over in the ear
It was natural to hear
Poetry with meter

Now the scene has seemed to change
Words that come are often strange
It is harder to arrange
Poetry with meter

Telling stories is a test
What's the word that says it best?
I am always on a quest
For Poetry with meter

Words in hiding as I age
Set new limits on the page
That's the challenge of this stage
Of Poetry with meter

# Gossip

As children we play "telephone"
And chuckle with delight,
When all our whispered messages
Are changed from day to night.

As grownups we forget it seems
When we've a tale to tell,
That once the words have left our lips,
The story seems to swell.

Recounted details get enlarged
While wisdom seems to fall,
The tale that was confided first
Is not the same at all.

This, then, is where the problem lies:
The truth was not expressed.
False facts assumed a larger role
Creating undue stress.

The glee we took, while telling tales
About another's pain,
Returns to haunt our social slip
And nullify the gain.

## Waiting

There is an art to waiting
And some know how it's done
Proclaimed by these adherents
"The War on Waiting's Won!"
I'll give you some examples
Of teachings drawn from life.
Some expert tested samples
Avoiding anxious strife.

Four varied situations
Herein will show you "How"
There's waiting in the future
Or in the here and now.
There's waiting for conditions.
There's waiting for your turn.
Some wait with premonition
Or wait to live and learn.

Miss Lucie had a neighbor
Equal to the task
Of having fun together,
Too shy, he feared to ask.
Miss Lucie found a reason
To pull a switch on FATE.
She went and rang the doorbell
And never had to wait!

Marvin was a sailor
Who sailed the seven seas.
His job was sighting icebergs
Reporting depth of freeze.
His mission was successful,
His waiting was no strain,
As icebergs in the tropics
Are really on the wane.

Belinda was a dancer
Her life was on the stage.
At seventy and counting
She never seemed to age.
Her order in the chorus
Was number twenty-four.
She knew her turn was coming
When they pushed her out the door.

And Peter had a project
A scientific way
To test the phrase that what goes up
Comes down without delay.
Pete threw a ball high in the air
And marveled at his fate;
As often as he tossed the ball
He never had to wait!

We envy these exemptions,
Techniques we'd like to know.
For most of us who have to wait
Can feel impatience grow.
If we are stuck in traffic
Or forced to wait in line,
Our thoughts can turn quite graphic
When with curses they combine.

Delays for work appointments
Situations which cause stress
May result in new "conjoint"-ments,
That will lessen our success.
Or, again, upon reflection,
(Hoping for a day of fun),
Resurrect an old connection
For some playtime in the sun.

But the message we're retrieving
Says to wait for two days hence.
Are we ready for believing
We can deal with the suspense?
With our modern culture's turmoil
That we meet at every turn,
We expect our blood to boil
As we choose to grin and burn.

We know waiting is no pleasure
But it's how we pay our dues
And the privilege we treasure
Is to sing the "Waiter's Blues."

## Precious Sleep

Sleep grants us the gift of renewal
When we're weary and feeling forlorn.
Sleep can also dilute our remembrance
Permitting new strengths to be born.

Some sleep demands total commitment
No dreams or exertion takes place.
Compare it to death on the pillow
The sleeper beyond time and space.

It's not the deep sleep of an illness,
Nor one that is medically prescribed.
Arousal from this can be varied
Refreshed or subdued or revived.

Sleep also comes to us unbidden
When exhaustion surrenders its stand.
With stress our endurance decreases,
We submit to our body's command.

At times sleep is fitful and restless,
We dream of the problems unsolved.
Still blinded by flaws of perception,
Solutions are yet unresolved.

Let's not forget "dozing" or "snoozing,"
The raggle-tag offspring of sleep.
When time or conditions are meager,
We settle for what we can keep.

Again "forty winks" and the "power nap,"
Example of "catch as catch can."
Our sleep's such a powerful ally,
We'll take it without a set plan.

Lullabies provide peace for the singer,
As well as to whom songs are sung.
The rhythm seduces the sleeper
With serenity when we are young.

So we think childhood's slumber is peaceful
Yet, children's "night terrors" are real.
Their reserve of life's knowledge is scanty
And their fearful encounters "slow-heal."

And forget about sleeping for mothers
And children with lives on the run,
Escaping from death and disaster,
Seeking happiness under the sun.

For them such repose is a memory
Filled with yearning for sheltering arms.
They recall from a far distant lifetime
How they slept with protection from harm.

Precarious conditions surround us
Who live in the world of today.
They mirror our human emotions
As we live or we die or we pray.

In wartime the battlefields fire
And rockets that kill as men sleep
Conspire to eradicate dreaming
Of the Life we want so much to keep

Let's believe that our dreams help renewal
Of new visions and more restful sleep.
Let's remember how life seemed more peaceful
When all that we counted were sheep.

## Luxury

Every morning I awake
Which direction shall I take?
Life has granted me a choice.
All I have to do is voice
My amusement for the day.
Do I want to work or play?
Will I meet with friends for lunch,
Shop for bargains on a hunch?
Search and find for what I look,
Stay inside and read a book?
Think how lucky I can be
When all I need is to be me.

## Memories to Be Forgotten

There once was a fire in seventy-five.
Scenes from this episode barely survive
Events on this calm summer day did evolve
From blissful denial to frantic resolve.

Although it was summer, (the book was so good,)
It was autumn leaves burning, and not the house wood.
But black smoke that drifted downstairs from above
Forced horror to register rather than love.

The Fire Department arrived on the scene,
Delayed to inaction locating the means
To hook to the hydrant to put out the flame,
For not every fire is treated the same.

They entered the house from the farthest hotspot
And soaked lots of places where fire was not. . .
Soon furniture landed on lawn with a thump
And made house exterior look like a dump.

The neighbors came over and sat on the fence
And watched the proceedings with interest immense.
The owner, in nightgown, seen putting her pet
In the car far away where the smoke and hose met.

Local news carried tales how the fire began
By installing a new theft and smoke alarm plan.
This ironic development carried the day—
Faulty wiring meant that insurance would pay.

# Adjusting

*Author's note: The art of adjusting refers to any or all activity that is new and not yet accepted. "Moving" can refer to a physical relocation or the actual painful involvement of limbs and joints, or it can be a substitute for learning to swim, ski, etc.*

Oh! Moving is a grumble—
A jumble—
      And a "mumble"—
A stumble—
      And a tumble
'Til you get it right.


But hopefully you'll take it
Put on a grin and make it
Without the need to fake it
'Til you feel all right.

Life offers many changes
That's what the "Road" arranges
Get used to what the "strange" is
'Til it works out right.

# Hospital Vigil/Antidote

We absorb and adapt, accept and assume
As part of our "Bargain" with life.
The myriad masterings we will perform
For being exempted from strife.

But none are immune and all get a share
Which arrive unannounced one fine day.
If we're old or we're young, if we're ready or not
Strife "portions" out "samples" our way.

Gratuitous "gifting" is rarely a "gain"
And rarely received with good grace.
The struggle within us that seeks to survive
Reminds us of what we must face.

*Antidote*

*Forsake dwelling inward. Recall how to love.*
*Strength comes from the choices we make.*
*Accepting each other while sharing ourselves*
*Frees a balm which might soothe our heart's ache.*

## Gourmet History

I took a look in my cookbook
To find out how to make it
I'd just recalled I'd been enthralled
And vowed that I would bake it.

As I engaged the yellow page
My memory was arrested
Because I found that "honor bound"
All "tastes" were truly tested.

The yearly tie for *Pumpkin Pie*
Brought back Thanksgiving dinner
Where it was learned and duly earned
Aunt Millie was the winner.

The New Year's toast to *Mom's Pot Roast*
And *Fluffy Dumplings* made it
The treat to seal tradition's meal
A joy when we obeyed it.

In spring there were the sponge cakes
All cousins would compete
To see whose cake was lightest
Aunt Joan's was never beat.

And there was Dave's chopped liver
Hors d'oeuvres beyond compare,
Muriel's stuffed Eggplant
And Jack's grilled steak, served rare.

Each index card was referenced
With name of Cook and Dish
Which aided repetition
Whenever one would wish.

Some cooks had long departed
This life for other lands
The beauty of this system
Was fame stayed in their hands.

Another unsought bonus
My recent search revealed
Was a gastronomic "memoir"
Where nothing was concealed.

Techniques discerned from knowledge earned
And tastefully ingested
Appeared in books for family cooks
Directly reinvested.

Dot's Apple Cake, Sue's Pepper Steak,
Jean's Frozen Blintz Soufflé,
Memorialized with honor
Forever and a day.

# Enough Already!

Around, around, and around I go
Into the shambles of thought,
Over the ledges and bramble bush hedges
I'm trapped by solutions I've sought.

On the one hand, I've captured a dream.
On the other hand, I'm in a ditch.
From heaven to bunker, I'm up or I'm down
Not knowing which pathway is which.

I'm stumbling around in the mud,
Conclusions are mired in doubt.
Enough of this feeling my way in the dark.
Oh! When will the sunshine come out?

# Tempus Fugit

"Tempus Fugit" so they say
What a great disaster!
We keep speeding up our lives
Helping us go faster.

We get in a race with Time
Thinking we will match up.
But he seems to sprint ahead,
We will never catch up.

There's a secret here to know,
His pace never changes.
As we age, our movements slow,
That's what life arranges.

## "Tempus" Tamed

When I was a child
My perspective was short
And a year stretched as far as a mile.
With my four-year-old stride
I could never decide
Would my birthday be soon or awhile?

And then I grew up
And perspective improved
And a mile or a year was a breeze.
Before I could figure
(Without too much vigor)
I'd accomplished them both with great ease.

But now that I'm older,
Most movements are slow.
Perspective has changed once again.
A year is a minute,
And all actions in it
Depend on the "If," "How," or "When."

Again Time goes by
And perspective is short,
And the hours are all mine to fill.
Time may well fly faster
**But now I'm the Master,**
**And I will decide what I will.**

# As Time Goes By:
## "Portraits of Departure"

### Departure 1:
### "Hi there, anyway"

They say it's hard for you to swallow.
They say it's hard for you to speak.
So I am hoping you will follow
These few lines when smiles you seek.

I'm not a jokester, all can tell you.
I forget the end-line punch.
But I sure could buy and sell you
Love and kisses by the bunch.
We have what is known as friendship.
Some are short but ours is long.
It keeps going with no "end-ship"
Day by day the bonds get strong.
Don't think you will ever lose me,
You can't make this friendship shrink.
If you think that would amuse me,
You should think another think.

Departure 2:
"Touch-Up"

Today
I will put in order
The things that need to be.
I will carefully arrange
The shades on my Eastern windows
So, looking out,
I will see the sun rise
In the Eastern sky.

I will take the books
On the Poetry Shelf
And stand them straight.
No leaning over
Upside down
For them.
When last did I need
To check out that rhyme?

And now,
I will smooth the pillow
Of seamless satin
That sits on my chair
That you gave to me.

There! That's better.

Departure 3:
"Hallowed Presence"

In the morning
It was still there.

The worried heaviness
And wide-awake awareness
Was still there….

It spoke to me
In murmured mutterings
And screamed in silence:

"She is dead!"
"She is dead!"
"She is no more…."

In the morning
It was still there.

It spoke to me
In murmured mutterings
And screamed in silence….

AN ABSENCE IS A PRESENCE!

Departure 4:
"Armageddon"

In the valley of my heart
In the caverns of my soul
I am living.

Love and friendship thrown apart
Shreds of life no longer whole.
Unforgiving.

Alone. Alone.
I am alone.
In my land.

Departure 5:
"Unexpected Farewells"
*For Sue Hyman*

Some go beyond their reach of time and space
And open up their dreams of life with hope.
They've wallowed in the depths of dark despair
And known the twists and knots of shadowed nights.
They've stretched to find the upward path that leads
Away from petty preference and pain.
They know within the truth of tempered thought
The life they seek is one they will attain.

# Backward Glance

To let the thoughts of yesterday arise
Now dressed in memory's sentimental hues
And see again those scenes before our eyes
Which falter with remembrance of those views.
Was this a dream or borrowed from a tale?
Did consciousness and daily life engage,
Or automatic chore-dom always fail
To recognize we lived as on a stage?

# Portraits

# The Call of Rusty Rustle

The silken rustle of her skirt
Swished on the kitchen floor.
Her high heels clacked across the room
And out the backyard door.

She called, "Goodbye!" But no one heard.
"So much for them," she thought.
She turned for one last farewell look
At what she once had sought.

Her back was straight, her footsteps firm.
She'd had her dreams of old,
But no one spoke to her of love
Her life felt bare and cold.

She'd lain awake nights hoping
Her dreams would all come true.
But time stretched on unchanging,
Her pleasures were too few.

She was alone, no more a child.
Her life was hers to live.
Inside she felt the promise
Of what she had to give.

"Go West, Young Man," said Greeley
But ladies, please stay home.
The hand that rocks the cradle,
Is not supposed to roam.

The train roared in the station,
Her ticket read "one-way."
She's on her way to somewhere,
But where she could not say.

She's seeking fame and fortune,
Adventure in her breast.
Her fears remain well-hidden
While she pursues her quest.

The frontier towns are noisy.
The frontier towns are wild.
The frontier is the homeland,
For those unreconciled.

She made her way with caution.
She learned what she must learn.
She's wise beyond her years soon
With no thought to return.

She changed her name to Rustle
And rustling was her game.
She stole the hearts of many,
Which brought her wealth and fame.

The town sprang up around her.
"There's gold in them thar hills!"
She bought a little gold mine
And opened up the stills.

The town elects her mayor.
She owns it; there's no doubt.
And travelers come by thousands
To see what gold's about.

A train pulls in the station.
A face she knows descends.
She watches from her window,
She thinks, "Can I be friends?"

He needs to borrow money.
He wants to stake a claim.
He ends up on her doorstep.
He does not know her name.

The years have changed her greatly.
The blond has turned to gray.
He wants to borrow money.
He swears he will repay.

She asks about his family
And what he left behind.
He answers, "There is no one
Except a wife who's blind."

"No children, then?" she prompts him.
His hand goes to his eyes.
"Not anymore," he murmurs.
"We know not where she lies.

She left us in the springtime,
Some twenty years ago.
We haven't heard nor seen her.
She vanished like the snow."

The woman's eyes grew thoughtful.
Her brain had formed a plan.
"I cannot lend the money
To just a single man."

"A man can be a drifter
And live a sordid life.
If you want money from me,
You must bring me your wife!"

The man's firm jaw dropped open,
"Of funding I'm bereft!"
"Here's money for the railroad."
He took her cash and left.

The train pulled in the station.
She watched them both descend.
They wait upon her doorstep.
She knows the feud must end.

They come into her chamber,
Their manner full of fear.
Their years sit heavy on them,
Her eyes begin to tear.

"Do you not know me, Mother?
Have you forgotten, Dad?
I am your long-lost daughter,
Too many years were sad."

"I had to leave your farmhouse.
Your life was not for me.
I knew that somewhere, someplace,
Was a place that I could be."

"I am now well and happy
I'm willing to forgive.
If you will say you've missed me,
We can go forth and live."

The frontier towns are noisy.
The frontier towns are wild.
The frontier towns are havens
For those unreconciled.

The message in this story
Is very plain to see
The song her soul was singing
Was the call of destiny.

# The Visionary

He was alone, tall, debonair, and stately
But not the first time he had felt this pain.
His life had always moved along sedately,
And now the emptiness was here again.

In youthful days he'd been a solemn soul
Observed and calculated what to plan.
He'd slow his pace to see the outcome whole,
While others risked or leapt to feel a man.

When love arrived, she swept him off his feet.
He'd energy and vision without end.
He knew that she would make his life complete.
And best of all, he'd truly have a friend.

And so they wed and loved and family grew
The bond between them deepened as he'd known.
When, unannounced, alarm obscured their view
Presaging their idyllic life had flown.[2]

---

[2] The auto-immune condition called "wasting disease" is caused by decreasing vascular supply, where the tissues lose nutrition because of lack of blood flow.

His pain would start when daytime lights would dim
And she could no more answer from her bed.
And then there was no other voice for him,
As quiet emptiness surrounded him with dread.

The years flew fast. The children left the home
The "emptiness" had changed, he now felt numb.
He still saw friends but had no wish to roam
He watched the seasons go and others come.

An old friend's sister moved to town with kids
Their needful antics re-awoke his role.
And he recalled enjoying what they did
And soon the numbness thawed and filled the hole.

He was too young to live alone, he thought
The woman was compatible and kind.
The children brought the joy that he had sought.
He wed and left the emptiness behind.

He was a gratefully recovered man
His life and style now suitably restored.
Fate intervened to reinvent his plan
And took his wife with stroke. She lived no more.

The loneliness took hold and he withdrew.
A colleague saw him change and set a trap.
He made a plan for two with lands to view.
For "her," about a Treasure Island map.

For "him," a case of properties for sale.
The "upshot" was that each became confused.
To clarify the "mix-up" of this tale
Two strangers met and soon became amused.

There was no doubt, these two were worlds apart.
When one would laugh, the other thought it strange.
And yet, a friendship did begin to start
And meetings seemed important to arrange.

Together they began to speak of life
And how, at times, their lives felt incomplete.
Each shared their loss of husband and of wife
And how they'd lived before they chanced to meet.

She was a runner and involved in sports,
There'd been no children (not her plan by choice.)
She was a lawyer, and well known in courts
As advocate for children with no voice.

He told his life and loss of loved ones gone
And marveled at her strength and will to give,
And how his kids compelled him greet each dawn
If not for them, he'd had no will to live.

An interesting case of unmet needs
With children as a focus for them both.
The properties involved proved to be "seeds"
A resource for some children's further growth.

For him, it was a "country-farm" type school.
For her, it was a "Treasure Island" camp.
They found their ideas close enough to "pool"
And felt that "Fate" approved them with its stamp.

Twelve years have passed. It functions on its own.
Endowments sought to subsidize their plan
Their innovative model[3] stands alone,
A tribute to the Woman and the Man.

---

[3] This poem, about a visionary who started a school, was inspired by the novels *Little Men* and *Life at Plumfield with Jo's Boys*, written by American author Louisa May Alcott. The events in this are not to be confused with the real-life history of Louisa May Alcott's father, Amos Bronson Alcott, who was also a visionary and leader in education.

In reality, Amos Bronson Alcott established successful unconventional schools based on transcendental philosophy. "In 1834 Alcott opened a school for thirty pre-teenage boys and girls in The Masonic Temple in Boston. The founding of the Temple School in Boston was Bronson's most famous educational experiment. . .the children ranged in age from six to twelve years old." www.alcott.net/alcott/home/education.html. The novels *Little Men* and *Life at Plumfield with Jo's Boys* tells the story of the children at her father's school. The story of Amos Bronson Alcott can be found at www.alcott.net/alcott/home/education.html.

The man now took the time to track his tale,
And learn the story of his parent's life,
Who perished when the "Healer" could but fail
Diphtheria's dying husband and his wife.

Alone, afraid, and missing parent's care
The child, at three, was sent to live with friends.
He did not understand why he was there
And hoped the "mixed-up" times would finally end.

The friends were kind. He knew they loved and cared
And yet, he felt a "missing space" inside.
He found it eased when there were things he shared
He learned to "fill the hole" when e're he tried.

The school plus camp had been a dream fulfilled
A loving sharing home had been his goal.
A haven waiting for someone to build
Which spoke to him from deep within his soul.

# Field of Dreams

The cornfields of the West were home
He loved the land's expanse.
Where seasons chose how life was lived
With little left to chance.

By day he led an ordered life
The pattern hardly changed.
The tasks and skills refined by time
Were rarely rearranged.

A quiet man with dreams to spare
And fairly free from strife.
The work he'd chosen gave him pride
He loved his child and wife.

He was a man of many dreams
He kept them in his head.
He thought about them when at rest
And when he slept in bed.

As years passed by and work decreased,
The dreams instead grew grand.
He spent a larger part of time
Engrossed in Never-land.

The panoramic canvas hues
Of colors in the sky
Returned to him a sense of peace
And pleasure to his eye.

He fantasized himself with brush
And palette in his hand,
A Master Artist who could paint
The beauties of the land.

The spread of birds across the sky
Brought fantasies of flight.
He conjured up the rush of wind
And weightlessness of height.

From there imagination soared
He strove to understand
Effects that Nature's sounds produced
On creatures of the land.

When streaks of lightning crashed in air
Artistically displayed,
And thunder rumbled over plains,
Were lesser lives afraid?

The day's dreams differed from the nights',
The night-time scenes felt real.
He pondered on the startling fact
While sleeping, he could feel!

Such terrors faced when fast asleep
Such soulful love or pain
Aroused within his slumbering self
Thoughts he could not explain.

What line was crossed when this occurred?
Sensation was the key.
How visions drifted from the mind
To Soul was mystery.

In early years of work-filled life
The seasons were his guide
And Nature formed the work-day's plan
That kept his dreams inside.

But now, as older years advanced,
Another thought emerged,
Man's life, itself, had seasons.
On this all truths converged.

His life approaching winter-time
An urgency began.
With no more need for "splinter-time"
His mind conceived a plan....

*"Release and share those cloistered dreams*
*And free the inner man."*

# Sonnet to M[4]

How are you special? Just recall the ways
You welcome life and greet it at the door,
Deciding in your heart with each new phase
That you'll accept whatever is in store.

You came alone. From horror newly freed
And faced new language, customs, friends, and kin.
Embracing your intention to succeed
You opened up your heart and let them in.

Much wisdom came through trials both great and small,
Loves won and lost too soon. Achievements grew.
Your book and lectures testify to all
That live with "menshlachkeit"* is what you do.

So celebrate! Give honor to your years.
May Future's gift be love and hope, not tears.

* *"Menshlachkeit" is the Yiddish term for "humanitarian."*

---

[4] "A sonnet is fundamentally a dialectical construct which allows the poet to examine the nature and ramifications of two usually contrastive ideas, emotions, states of mind, beliefs, actions, events, images, etc., by juxtaposing the two against each other, and possibly resolving or just revealing the tensions created and operative between the two." ~Nelson Miller, www.sonnets.org/basicforms.htm
"Sonnet to M" follows the traditional Shakespearian Sonnet form of abab/cdcd/efef/gg.

# The Odyssey[5]

*Author's note: This is a Portrait of an unexpected change in plans and the ensuing loving and welcomed result. Complete with chorus and refrain. Format and rhythm adapted from Dr. Seuss's* Horton Hatches the Egg.

*Chorus:*
*Cyndi and Randy, Randy and "Cyd"*
    *Just listen to all that those two people did!*

They came for a visit
To spread love and cheer
But never imagined
That work would appear
As part of vacation
To such a degree
That sights for a tourist
They never would see.

They were willing and eager
And "loaded for bear"
With not one idea
Of the work they would share!

---

[5] Format and rhythm adapted from Dr. Seuss's *Horton Hatches the Egg*, Random House Books for Young Readers (October 12, 2004).

*Chorus (If desired) (whispering is good)*
*. . . Cyndi and Randy, Randy and "Cyd"*
   *Just listen to all that those two people did. . .*

The first task made known
In an offhand remark
Was to "liberate" treasures
Two years in the dark
Well hidden in closets
In stack after stack
Were boxes to carry
Downstairs and unpack.

Mountains of newspapers slowly appeared
Along with the objects so greatly revered.
Each wrapping was smoothed
And each box broken flat.
Recycling's the rule,
That's where these folks were at.

Next on the agenda
Phone calls to be made,
Exploring the options
For debts to be paid.
They divided the labor
Each one had a part,
Then Randy made phone calls
And Cyd made a chart.
The chart was a flow sheet
To give me a clue,
For what was the schedule
When all bills came due.
To change the procedure
for paying the bills
I'll soon do it "auto"
And cure all my ills.

(My math teacher's cheering
Is heard in the hills)

And Randy showed patience
the envy of saints,
"phone-waiting" for hours
With no real complaints.

Are you thinking that's all?
You are wrong, you will see.
Technology items
Kept secrets from me.
But Randy revealed them
(Cyd opened the door.)
She took notes in detail,
I'm stymied no more.
I can now play T.V.,
Thermostat is my friend.
I'm viewing in comfort—
"cool" cat to the end.

And if there were moments
When Cyndi might rest,
She'd "dead-head" the flowers
With zeal and with zest.
Then Randy took charge of
Garage's "makeover"—
Helped re-load the pod
So no junk would take over.
Cyd helped with the cooking,
Both cleaned up the mess.

'Twas useless to argue
While under duress.
(A "two-person" face off
Could <u>really</u> *cause stress*.)

Next they shopped and they schlepped,
They "toted that bale."
They were better than elves
From the shoemaker's tale.
And when all's said and done
At the end of their stay,
We could say we had fun
In a full-hearted way.
There was love all around
Or I'm crazed as a bat,
Who else would commit
To vacation like that?


*Chorus (If desired) (whispering is good)*
*. . . Cyndi and Randy, Randy and "Cyd"*
       *Just listen to all that those two people did. . .*

So you see what I mean
Why this ode was begun,
For these wonderful folks
On this side of the sun.
And I'm sure as can be
There are items I've missed
As I'm making up rhymes
To add on to this list.
But this poem is long
You'll agree—just recall
If I've skipped a few deeds
I give thanks for them all.

"I meant what I said
And I said what I meant"
These folks are terrific
One-hundred percent![6]

*Chorus (No if's, and's or but's this time. . .OUT LOUD! )*
*. . . Cyndi and Randy, Randy and "Cyd"*
     *Just listen to all that those two people did. . .*

---

[6] Ibid., adapted from Dr. Seuss, *Horton Hatches an Egg*, page 16.

## The Friend

At first the tone is light and airy,
To live and know what's coming
Secure and safe from harm,
To keep her lifestyle careful
With no need for alarm.
To wake with calm each morning
And never have to hear
Intrusive interruptions
Portending psychic fear.

This was her planned ambition.
She thus arranged her life.
Rejecting all distractions
Including that of wife.
Her week's routine was simple
Repeated day by day,
She planned her working hours,
She planned when she would play.

Companions she befriended
Accepted her decrees
Within her social limits
She was not hard to please.
Life gave her one exception
She had not planned for that.
One day upon her threshold
She found a Pussy Cat!

Of course the cat was hungry
And soon began to cry.
Before she thought, she fed it
And never wondered why.
The kitten was a charmer
And soon began to purr.
One fact impressed the woman
The cat had chosen *her*!

Invited as a housemate,
On trial or to admit.
They lived within their boundaries
Or met as each saw fit.
She felt a bond between them
As each determined how
To satisfy their basic needs
Within the here and now.

The adoption proved successful
And trust began to grow
As each enjoyed companion time,
The woman's fears let go.
Of course there were "distractions,"
The cat was lost or sick. . . .
Locked in a storage closet
And needing action quick.

Or, consulting with a Doctor,
(Unconscious cat in arms)
The fear of its extinction
Reviving past alarms.
The difference with these new events
When frantic times were past
The well-planned life resumed again
But new fears did not last.

So peace returned and time went on
The two became a pair.
They sought each other out at night
And sat in one big chair.
As they grew old and time moved on,
Some fifteen years passed by.
The woman saw with heavy heart
That soon her cat would die.

The thought of loss did not cause fear
Instead, she now felt bad.
She recognized that she had changed
And realized she felt sad.
And when, at last, her cat did die
Her grief was great and deep.
Emotions that were now released
Permitted her to weep.

In war-torn world when she was six
Her mother said with fright,
*"Run quickly to the wood-shed*
*And don't come out 'til night.*
*No matter what, you stay inside,*
*No matter what you hear. . . ."*
She knew not why, but she obeyed
And stayed there with her fear.

At night she crept back to her house
But not a soul was there.
For two long days she lived with hope
While trembling with despair.
At last she walked the mile or so
To neighbors that she knew.
They told her that her folks were jailed
Proclaiming treason's view.

She never cried when she was six,
She kept it all inside.
Her head knew all that happened,
Her feelings had to hide.
Now living safely with her cat
And feeling loved within,
Despite her loss, she felt at peace
And new ways could begin.

# Renaissance

For years they lived together side by side,
They woke and ate and worked and slept in bed.
They shared their dreams and counted out the years
And marveled how their world changed since they'd wed.

They never noticed changes in themselves
The wrinkled skin or slow and halting gait.
They only sensed that something great had gone
And slowly felt their joy evaporate.

The woman chose to wander in the woods
She watched the seasons come and seasons go.
She had no sense of wonder as before
When appetites were whet by Nature's glow.

When she looked up, the view was dark and grim;
It seems all light had vanished from the skies.
When she looked down, the ground beneath was black;
She looked away and slowly closed her eyes.

And then she saw a vision in her head,
A lovely creature never seen before
Half child-half sprite and beautifully formed,
Adorned in lustrous raiment as of yore.

The woman stood transfixed upon the spot.
The beauty and the radiance of the scene
Were mesmerizing, filling her with awe,
Transporting her to where she'd never been.

A sigh or cry escaped from deep within.
The vision smiled and beckoned her advance.
As she approached, she lost all sense of time
Submitting to the Destiny of Chance.

Now face to face, locked in each other's gaze,
They seemed to draw from one another's soul.
The woman felt a surge of new-born strength
Returning her to life and make her whole.

The lovely creature now appeared to gain
An air of deeper empathy and thought.
The impish sense of innocence remained,
To wit and charm a blended whole was brought.

The man at home relaxed before the fire.
His pain was eased when staying off his feet.
The way he lived was farthest from desire
In every way his life felt incomplete.

When in his prime he'd golfed and swam and ran,
There was no sport that he had never tried.
He always was a strong and healthy man
And he was sure he'd stay so 'til he died.

Now dozing off and dreaming of the past,
A vision interjected in his brain.
He saw himself erect and free at last
And dreamed he'd died and would not live again.

A loneliness arose to flood his soul,
Recalling tearful nights from early years.
To save himself and help himself feel whole,
He'd chosen sports to soothe and calm his fears.

When he was three his mother died one day,
His father moved and never did come back.
Some family came and took him far away
And no one even tried to help him pack.

Now deep in sleep and feeling all alone,
An insight flashed! He understood his dream.
His youthful isolation fears had flown
When he became a member of a team.

Discovery felt good but incomplete,
For each there was a greater need to share.
A need for mirrored love and pride for growth
As witnessed by the eyes and ears that care.

He could not wait to tell her of his dream
How being in the grave was just return
To loneliness, for nowhere would he learn
About her world when *they* were not a team.

For her, the joy again rose in her heart.
The need for affirmation was her core.
She'd known her contribution from the start
She was his root in solid ground, forevermore.

# The Winner

She rose at dawn,
Her tasks were few.
She knew exactly
What to do.
She milked the cow.
She fed the hens.
She took the mash
Out to the pens.
Then on the stove
She put the pan
And started breakfast
For her man.
Today at last
The time had come.
She'd win the prize
Collect the sum.
Her entry always
Pleased the judge
Who had a sweet tooth for her fudge.

*Recalling as the door was latched*
*"Do not count chickens till they're hatched."*

# The Milk Train

The phone call came at five o'clock,
He still was in his room.
He heard the pay-phone in the hall,
A harbinger of doom.

The last four years had been too hard;
He'd lived a lonely life.
Before that fateful summer,
He'd had a child and wife.

It's not that they had lived and died
That would have made an end.
But circumstances had contrived
His good life to suspend.

His marriage now in name alone,
Each living miles apart.
She lived confined behind locked doors,
He lived with broken heart.

And, when they met, the past was gone.
She neither spoke nor moved
And countless visits just confirmed
That nothing had improved.

His funds were sparse; his jobs were scarce.
No home could he provide.
The family took the child to heart
And kept their grief inside.
They planned: two cousins, close in age,
Might help a new life start.

The girl, now nine, was doing well,
Some sorrow did abate.
But life could not continue
And he could only wait.

Day after day, year after year,
His routine carried on.
He taught his class and went to school,
No goals to build upon.

He saw the child just once a week,
He never missed the day.
She was his only anchor
For where the future lay.

And yet he could not disengage,
The past still held him tied.
He could not fathom what occurred
And how their lives applied.

No answer came from anywhere.
The truth was still not known.
He dwelt inside a no-man's-land
From whence all life had flown.

Then came the phone call in the hall,
Alarm raged stem to stern.
Concerning information
He'd never dreamed he'd learn.

His daughter, now a summer guest
With relatives upstate,
Was diagnosed for surgery
With little time to wait.

Permission was required first,
With papers to be signed.
But how to get from here to there
Was what he had to find.

In '38, night options few,
The milk train ran that route.
With countless stops along the way
And no room for dispute.

Six hours on a midnight train
That "shuckled" to and fro
And offered too much time to think
Which way his fate would go.

A poem from his youth returned,
"The Erl-King" was its name.
Its focus was on life and death.
His focus was the same.

As dawn arrived, he signed his name,
The surgeon could begin.
His child lay in the balance,
Which fate for her would win?

At ten o'clock a nurse appeared
To take him to her bed.
A childish form so small and still
At first he thought her dead.

But then she sighed, and then she moved
She opened up her eyes.
"Why, Daddy, how come you're <u>here</u>?"
She asked with great surprise.


*Author's note: "The Erl-King" by Johann Wolfgang von Goethe
is reprinted here in its entirety as an illustration of the man's
memory and experience referred to as his "milk train" ride.*


## The Erl-King

Johann Wolfgang von Goethe
*www.poemhunter.com/poem/the-erl-king*


WHO rides there so late through the night dark and drear?
The father it is, with his infant so dear;
He holdeth the boy tightly clasp'd in his arm,
He holdeth him safely, he keepeth him warm.

"My son, wherefore seek'st thou thy face thus to hide?"
"Look, father, the Erl-King is close by our side!
Dost see not the Erl-King, with crown and with train?"
"My son, 'tis the mist rising over the plain."

"Oh, come, thou dear infant! oh come thou with me!
Full many a game I will play there with thee;
On my strand, lovely flowers their blossoms unfold,
My mother shall grace thee with garments of gold."

"My father, my father, and dost thou not hear
The words that the Erl-King now breathes in mine ear?"
"Be calm, dearest child, 'tis thy fancy deceives;
'Tis the sad wind that sighs through the withering leaves."

"Wilt go, then, dear infant, wilt go with me there?
My daughters shall tend thee with sisterly care
My daughters by night their glad festival keep,
They'll dance thee, and rock thee, and sing thee to sleep."

"My father, my father, and dost thou not see,
How the Erl-King his daughters has brought here for me?"
"My darling, my darling, I see it aright,
'Tis the aged grey willows deceiving thy sight."

"I love thee, I'm charm'd by thy beauty, dear boy!
And if thou'rt unwilling, then force I'll employ."
"My father, my father, he seizes me fast,
Full sorely the Erl-King has hurt me at last."

The father now gallops, with terror half wild,
He grasps in his arms the poor shuddering child;
He reaches his courtyard with toil and with dread,
The child in his arms finds he motionless, dead.

*"'The Erl-King' by Johann Wolfgang von Goethe (1749-1832) German poet, playwright, novelist and natural philosopher is best known for his two-part poetic drama Faust (1808-1832), which he started around the age of twenty-three and didn't finish till shortly before his death sixty years later. He is considered one of the greatest contributors of the German Romantic period."*
*Reference: www.online-literature.com/goethe.*

# All's Well, Sweet Dreams

"Sweet Dreams," she said, as she kissed "goodnight."
"Sweet Dreams," she said, as she shut the light.
"Sweet Dreams," she smiled, as her fears took flight,
And she went about her living.

"All's well," she said, when her work was done.
"All's well," she said, to the setting sun.
"All's well," she said, left the "only one"
And she saw the seasons changing.

"Love lives," she said, as she grew old.
"Love lives," she said, when her home was sold.
"Love lives," she said, as she turned cold
And they laid her in her coffin.

"Poor soul," they said, as they stood and wept.
"Poor soul," they said, of the thoughts they kept.
"Poor soul," they said, then went home and slept,
But they never really knew her.

# Legacy

She was a lovely, kind, warm-hearted woman.
She lived across the road up near the mill.
She always had a cheerful thing to talk about,
And she would wave when coming 'round the hill.

We really didn't know too much about her
Except that she had moved from out-of-state.
She had a gently drawling Southern accent
That some in town just loved to imitate.

The Spring she came, we'd just survived a flood.
The shores and streets and grounds were all a mess.
She asked around where she could be of use
And pitched right in to help ease the distress.

When Summer ended people knew her name,
They helped her find a job at Sherman's store.
She fit right in and was a big success,
And all surmised she'd done that work before.

As time went on she bought a little house
Across the road right up there near the mill.
She settled in and joined events in town.
If not for Spring-time floods she'd be there still.

She lived alone and folks soon wondered why
A woman in her forties made a plan
To choose a life involving work and friends,
But not including children or a man.

She proved to be a rather private type,
Disdaining gossip as a social sport.
But people liked her well enough to choose
Her joining them for fun times she'd support.

And so she lived among us twenty years
And rarely did she leave or go away
On trips to special places on the map
Except when she would leave each year in May.

We never knew just where she went or why
We guessed an anniversary from the life
That she had lived before she came to town
And had endured with sorrow and with strife.

Last year the Spring-time floods returned again,
The pummeling pelt of rain was more severe.
The slippery soil-topped shale turned into clay,
Cascading down the hills and causing fear.

The land and rocks and rain came tumbling down
And loosened smaller houses in the way.
Her home was shoved by debris from the mill
And slid on soil-slick-shale into the bay.

One month after her death a man came 'round.
He asked and gave some facts about her life.
We learned that she'd been principal of a school
And that she'd been a mother and a wife.

Her family had been killed one stormy night
Returning from a Boy Scout Jamboree.
A jack-knifed trailer truck side-swiped their car
And slammed it off the bridge into the sea.

Her life was then transformed by misery,
The shock and grief remained beyond repair.
Her loss of two young sons and cherished mate
Meant that she found no solace anywhere.

Her husband's sister yearned to be a "Mom"
But Doctors said her body was a tomb.
The wish for newborn life inspired a plan:
To give a healthy haven in a womb

The three involved consulted with a team
Who all confirmed that Science could consent,
And thus the memory of loved-ones lost
Would live in life as had been their intent.

Next May, a baby girl was born with love
Surrounding her were three, whose joy was great
The mother, father, and the grateful heart
Of one who gave them cause to celebrate.

The woman now felt free to leave at last
Before she could not go, nor could she stay.
But now she left with peace inside her heart
And promised to come back each year in May.

Instead of untold memories of doom
She left behind a tale of life in bloom.

## Mix or Match

*How can it be?*, the woman said
*I am the same one still.*
Her eyes were moist, her tone annoyed,
A friend had served her ill.
It was unfair. It felt as if
Her essence was reproved
From bonds built slowly year by year
The warmth of love removed.

*And yet,* (her inner voice went on)
*I am the same one still.*
*A young girl whom I barely know*
*Sings praises I can't fill.*
*I have to know* (the woman said),
*The truth of who I am*
*Is it a fact that deep inside*
*My life is just a sham?*

As time went by, the anguish grew
The loss absorbed her life.
Connecting in with bygone pain
Revived an ancient strife.
Her fear was that the world could see
Some knowledge not her own
And thus she'd always be at risk
Of being left alone.

What really was invisible
And kept her in despair,
Was a presumption only she
Could effect true repair.
Negating deep emotion which
She did not comprehend,
She by-passed all the signals
Of a way to reach her friend.

Her "challenged" friend was ill awhile,
Prognosis was unknown.
The trauma of those dreadful years
She wished she could disown.
When mirrored memories reappeared
She found a fail-safe style
And withdrew deep inside herself
To stay there for awhile.

And, what about that younger girl
The woman hardly knew
Who praised the woman to the heights
With awe and honor due?
That troubled creature had a son
Whose care consumed her heart.
She thought to learn the source of strength
Our woman could impart.

This was the situation then
Three people cast adrift.
Each impacting the other one
Creating further rift.
And none aware of how their styles
Decreased their chance to gain
The very thing to fill the void
So love would still remain.

Our woman had a history
Of shouldering each task
She volunteered to be of aid
Without the need to ask.
Her strength lay in the role she lived
Her self-respect was strong.
As long as she could feel in charge,
She'd help you all day long.

Thus when the friend learned to retreat
To save <u>herself</u> from gloom,
Of course, our woman never took
This stance as "needing room."
But longer time spent "out of touch"
Aroused our woman's ire,
For fear of loss and love which meant
The solitude so dire.

And now conceive how this insult
The longer it took place,
Mirrored for each the very fear
They wanted to erase.
And know just how the young girl's plight
And desperate outreach
Would be delayed until the two
Had healed their tragic breach.

Projected onto Nations
This meld of Mix or Match,
A prize for Peaceful Unions
Is one we'd wish they'd "hatch."
Where all would dwell together
And Children would grow tall
And live in Peace and Friendship
With Harmony for All.

Snowtime
*for Ann*

*Preamble:*

*And summer left*
*And winter came.*
*For days snow fell*
*And fierce winds blew.*
*A white mist formed*
*That whirled and froze,*
*Around the forms*
*That marred its path.*

A pristine hush prevailed when calm returned.
All marveled at the sights their eyes beheld.
Strange monolithic signs of Nature's Art,
That dazzled viewers' vision in the sun.
The most impressive measured twelve yards high.

It stood alone apart from other forms,
As if to lead a stand of nearby trees.
And day by day each person checked its height
To verify its presence still remained.
It seemed a metaphor for man's pure hope.

As weeks went by the snow began to melt,
Familiar landmarks once again appeared.
A game began to guess what lay beneath
Such artistry as winter had bestowed.
What hid inside the lone one no one knew.

The mode in winter was to walk eyes down
Avoiding blustery wind and icy paths.
But no one left his home without the glance
In the direction of the icy shaft
To reaffirm its undiminished form.

It symbolized a strength and will to live,
Despite the knowledge of a certain death.
And people passing by recalled the times,
The challenges their own lives had survived.
And people hoped, in secret, it would last.

That winter saw a change in hearts of men.
A miracle took place inside their souls.
The beauty of the Arctic Artist's touch
Combined with wisdom that recalled their strength,
And lasted way past Springtime's gentle breath.

# "Unhand Me, Madam"[7]

## Part 1

She was my constant companion.
I never felt I was alone.
She lived by my side in the daytime,
At night she would call on the phone.

What began as a challenging friendship
With interests in common explored
Soon flared into "Funtime Forever"
With solitude seldom restored.

On weekends she'd make plans for outings
Insisting that I come along.
I tried to withstand her entreaties,
Response to refusal was strong.

Her voice had a whispered finality
Ensnaring decisions to change.
Volition was subject to capture,
I'd cancel the plans I'd arrange.

---

[7] "Unhand Me, Madam" is a title adapted from *Hamlet* Act I, Scene 4, Line #4, "Unhand me, gentleman."

At last came a sad recognition,
My old life was shrinking in space.
It seemed I'd been living in dreamland,
Enthralled while my life would erase.

I woke to my drowning identity,
No longer was I who I'd been.
Escape was my instant decision,
Retreat was the best way to win.

Withdrawal a declared intention
A painful but vital release,
To return to my prior prescription
My time spent alone must not cease.

**Part II**

Scene shifts:
Man now speaks to therapist…

"So here I am. I don't know why I'm here.
I think I need some help in how to end.
I wake each morning face to face with fear
I want to know how I can lose a friend.

"There was a time we liked to meet and talk
And there were times we'd only take a walk.
And there were weeks we'd never even meet,
Unless we saw each other on the street.

"But all at once she started with the phone
And she would call to ask was I alone.
And next she'd call and want to take a trip,
A week-end-holiday onboard a ship.

"Then I began to feel that I was trapped
And then I felt that something in me snapped.
I was no longer who I'd been before.
I do not know how I can shut the door."


**Part III**

Therapist reflects…

"So here's a paradox that you confront,
An interesting problematic stunt.
It's really fairly simple to resolve
You're closer when some distance is involved.
As long as you remember this is so,
You're free to live your life and come and go.

"You're not the only one who likes his space.
And therefore choose to live a slower pace.
But if you ever wish to ease the pain,
Come back, and we can look at it again."

# Metamorphosis

On the worn, scarred slabs of pavement
In the city's summer street,
She absorbed the skills of childhood
How to join and then compete.

In the Springtime there was hopscotch.
There was jump rope in the fall.
Sleds and snowballs in the winter.
Sidewalk games were best of all.

"Mother, May I?" was a winner
"Statues," "Red Light," "Bounce the Ball,"
"A," "My Name Is," for the skillful,
Played till dark and mother's call.

Growing up in concrete canyons
These were pleasures without pall.
And, as years rolled on relentless,
These were treasures she'd recall.

Time moves on, lifestyles evolving.
Now her children's lives bring news.
Not for them the concrete canyons,
Mountain canyons greet their views.

On a ranch in Colorado,
Spacious meadows all around,
Not for miles another neighbor,
Livestock noises softly sound.

In the winter through the snowdrifts
Signs of hoofprints on the ground.
In the spring new life continues,
Nature's rhythm most profound.

She contrasts her own beginnings
With her grandchild's vast surround,
And, amazed, she buys a pony
Feeling freedom newly found!

# Changing Times: Penetrating the Imponderable

# What is the Matter With Homeless Today?[8]

*Author's note: This was written in response to the August 26, 2013,* New York Times *article "Southern Capital Seeks New Limits on Homeless: City Council of Columbia Urges New Approach to Southern Hospitality"* [9]

*What* is the matter with Homeless today?
They're standing around and they don't go away.
They're blocking the sidewalks and get in the way.
What *is* the matter with Homeless today?

*What* is the matter with Homeless today?
They're waiting for shelters which won't make them pay.
On line, they shout curses and smoke while they stay.
What *is* the matter with Homeless today?

*What* is the matter with Homeless today?
There's a plan to remove them fifteen miles away.
'Cause folks driving cars don't feel safe if they stay.
What *is* the matter with Homeless today?

---

[8] Rhythmic rhyme scheme and meter inspired by and adapted from "Rice Pudding" by A. A. Milne, *When We Were Very Young* (New York: American Book-Stratford Press, 1924; reprint, New York: Dutton, 1954).

[9] Poem inspired by Alan Blinder, "Southern Capital Seeks Limits on Homeless," *New York Times*, August 26, 2013, p. A15. "In South Carolina's capital, officials declare that their tree-lined Main street, clogged with shops, banks, restaurants and hotels, is evidence that a long-sought-economic revival has arrived.... Business owners sounding increasingly worried about the threat that they believe the homeless pose to Columbia's economic surge, the City Council approved a plan this month that will essentially evict them from downtown streets."

*What* is the matter with Homeless today?
The city wants space for new jobs which will pay.

With *more* Homeless workers squeezed out of the fray,
And "JAIL TIME FOR VAGRANTS TRESPASSING" delay
Empathic solutions that deal with dismay.
Now *that's* what's the matter with Homeless today!

## The Voting Public

There are those men whose view is small,
Who live behind a mental wall.
They rarely challenge what they hear
And this way keeps them free of fear.

But news events from far and near
Inject confusion should they hear
Disasters, when they're caused by man,
Are not "ordained" as nature's plan.

And there are many who resist
The current trends all know exist.
Who rail against in thought and deed
What most agree is what we need.

And many claim all men are brothers,
(Except for those they see as "others.")
While those who doubt and can't "believe"
Think all conspire to deceive.

With such a mélange in our midst
The truth will surely not be missed
When everyone holds his own view,
While hoping you will join him, too.

# Signs of the Times

*Preamble:*

*There is a curt indifferent streak*
*Emerging in our midst*
*The manner seems withholding*
*And patience feels dismissed*

*The milk of human kindness*
*Is slower now to pour*
*We're heading down a pathway*
*We've never been before*

## NEWS ALERT!

Our "flavor" is changing!
We are moving toward "spicy and dicey."

No more "Mellow Fellow,"
Longtime friend of mine.
Where ever did all the years go?
We used to shoot baskets,
In Spring we'd take hikes.
Now we hardly have time for "hello."

# The New Way: Multi-Media Monster

*Preamble:*

*Demands increase in daily life*
*Our leisure seems to fade*
*Small talk with friendly neighbors*
*Seems to get delayed*

*Our new relaxing time is spent*
*In the old easy chair—*
*It takes the pressure out of life*
*When we just have to stare*

Oh, come all ye faithful, and let's watch T.V.
Just what is the special tonight?
It is Zola the Queen and her zombie-machine
Zooming in from the next satellite.

Or maybe the channel of choice is the one
With the menacing Monster Parade.
The artists conceive it, and viewers believe it
When villainous acts are displayed.

The Monsters are green-eyed and crave all they see
They make plans with evil intent.
They're greedy and grabby, they cheat and they're crabby
With failed schemes they helped to invent.

The Monsters are waiting with breath that's abating,
They're looking for money that's free.
It's fun ridiculing the people they're fooling.
Who cares who that happens to be?

The Monsters betray unsuspecting spectators
Their motto is: "Buyer Beware!"
They're not sympathetic; their morals, pathetic—
They're playing with those in despair.

Our lives are connected and surely affected
By monsters in life or T.V.
We don't want to see it—we're sure we can't be it
But—they're human like you and like me!

*Author's note: The second half of this poem is written in anapestic meter. Anapest is a three-syllable metrical foot that is made up of two unaccented syllables followed by an accented syllable. For example, the words "consequence" and "interlude" are anapestic. For more information on meter and rhythm schemes, see* The Poet's Manual and Rhyming Dictionary. *(Thomas Y. Crowell Company, 1965), or visit www.writing.upenn.edu/~afilreis/88v/meter.html.*

# Multi-Media Monsters 2:
# Cartoons for Four-Year-Olds

*Preamble:*

*We've just read the type of the topic and "hype"*
*In the usual grown adult fare.*
*But some children's "slot-time" mix cartoons with "plot time"*
*We need to be told to "Beware"*

*The message is clear: teach the children to fear*
*Anyone who is different than we.*
*They're mean and they're scary, we'd better be wary*
*It's not what we want kids to see.*

**Saturday Morning Cartoons?**

Young children play ball in a pool
And swim in the water that's blue.
Live sea-life of various types share the space,
All friends having fun what they do.

Now, Asian cartoon men come into the pool.
They're dressed in Kimonos with ties.
All carry long sticks that appear to do tricks
As kids watch for a "tricky" surprise.

Surprise! The blue water turns red!!
Dead sea-life floats up to the top. . .
The children get tearful, and many get fearful
When nobody makes the men stop.

This episode happens <u>three</u> times. . .
And children just wait "standing by."
Their play is invaded, not one child is aided.
Why should fun cartoons make them cry?

# Multi-Media Dating: Online Catfish[10]

*Preamble:*

*A rhyme? A chant? A good "Bon Mot"?*
*How best to help impact this phrase?*
*We're on our way to somewhere else*
*And stumbling through a maze.*
*Our lives may never be the same,*
*Try to eradicate this haze.*
*Let's now decide to designate*
*"catfished"…let's count the ways.*

A "catfish" is a sneaky fish who thrives on others' waste.
A scavenger with sucking lips, regarded with distaste.
In on-line dating, catfish means all secrets can be bared.
The naïve person takes the bait, unwittingly ensnared.

It's billed as "ideal for the internet age"
Facebooking dates people will try…
People want love so badly, despite ending sadly
They'll even make friends with a lie.

---

[10] "Catfish are a serious problem in online dating. Catfish are people who pretend to be someone they are not online. They create false IDs in order to pursue deceptive online romances. They can string people on for years and apparently, have no remorse for their actions." http://answers.yahoo.com/question/index?qid=20121122140149AARD1Aq.

It makes life quite risky and not always frisky
You're appraised by the World on the air.
Is it true you are you? Or just playing for fun?
Take your place in the sun if you dare.

Some victims are "catfished" resulting in stress
While others are riddled with fear.
Some people pursue it to find out "who knew it"
Then shamed to see how they appear.

# Ode to Manti Te'o: Catfished[11]

*Preamble:*

*A Football Star from Notre Dame*
*was trapped inside a hoax*
*That left him sad and feeling bad,*
*the naïve butt of jokes.*

Our story involves a young athlete of fame
Who was up for awards and was "hooked"
By a phone call received from a "woman" online
That authorities all overlooked.

A romance began with his online 'true-love'
(Manti T'eo was all in a swoon.)
In time she revealed she was terribly ill,
And said, "I'll be dying real soon."

Another shock came, that his *grandma had died*
Both losses before his big game.
"I'll play", so he said, "and I'll win it for them,
For my team and for my Notre Dame."

---

[11] Hollywood Reporter Manti Te'o, 'Catfish,' Katie Couric, Oprah and the Sports World: Paging Dr. Phil! http://www.hollywoodreporter.com/bastard-machine/manti-teo-story-hooks-media-415094.

For this he received many tributes believed
To be born of his strength and devotion.
But questions abound in this case all around
Resulting in lots of commotion.

Our linesman was *catfished*, a hero no more,
His character deemed to be flawed.
That noble endeavor and win for his school
Was accused of all matters of fraud.

When a student reported the Hoax to "N.D."
They then hired their own private team.
Then declined to continue on Te'o's behalf
For just how that endorsement might seem.

As press got involved, and the story evolved
There was little authorities knew.
Was this state of affairs just a sign no one cares
To investigate just what to do?

Besides the resistance to further assistance
These lucrative aspects appear
Many salaries depend that this culture not end
And cessation thereof brings much fear.

*Epilogue*

*Two hundred reporters bombard him with questions*
*Imbedded assumptions created congestions.*
*Asserting their viewpoints, in search of corruption,*
*No wonder his mind could not easily function.*

*Reporters who dug out details to explore*
*Then "razzed" him on gullible actions galore.*
*Omitting the very real crux of the case*
*The loss of his grandma and place in the race.*

# Multi-Media Sports Channel:
# Students Abused

*Author's note:*
*This was inspired by an article in the* Atlantic Magazine.

*Preamble:*

*The scourge has infiltrated sports*[12]
*Our recreation's boon.*
*We love to cheer what we call dear*
*On weekend afternoons.*
*But recently we're hearing*
*Deceptive tales most cruel*
*That are changing our perspective*
*(we yearn for some corrective)*
*Our sports were once reflective*
*Of our faith in golden rule.*

---

[12] "[T]he real scandal is the very structure of college sports, wherein student-athletes generate billions of dollars for universities and private companies while earning nothing for themselves. Here, a leading civil-rights historian makes the case for paying college athletes—and reveals how a spate of lawsuits working their way through the courts could destroy the NCAA. Taylor Branch, "The Shame of College Sports," *Atlantic Magazine*, October 11, 2011.

CⁿⓍⁿↃ

News stories are filled with dissension in schools
When the coaches have failed to correct
Unfair settlements made with team players dismayed
That result in the loss of respect.

Some coaches are fired, or early retired
When discovered to perpetrate sin.
While school Presidents lean toward ignoring the scene
As Alumni fund money to win.

Athletic Directors of prominent schools
Have many decisions to make.
Do they notify Press when confusion exists
Or seek other pathways to take?

Many theories abound when cruel hoaxes are found
Which impune and imply what is worst.
Do they notify law, or the NCAA[13]
Or decide to go privately first?

---

[13] The National Collegiate Athletic Association (NCAA) organizes college and university athletic programs.

# Students Speak Out

*Author's note: This was written in response to Taylor Branch, "The Shame of College Sports",* Atlantic Magazine, *October 11, 2011.*

The sports scene of late is enduring a fate
That it never envisioned could be.
Not <u>only</u> confusion because of delusion
That's shocking for all who can see.
But it seems students' dreams of advancing with teams,
Who trust salaries are fair from the start. . .
Are <u>ENRAGED</u> how the share of their earnings compare
With which profits the sponsors won't part.
*This scandal, it seems, interferes with their dreams*
*With these monies unfairly dispersed*
*those who need the worst should receive it the first*
*...so injustice can then be reversed*

Yoo hoo hoo! Remember Us Too…
And now we see what seems to be
The truth of what's at stake
The "aura of irrelevance"
And "sense of non-identity"
A student has to take.
How truly cruel and punishing,
Impertinent and blind,
Ignoring students' anguish
As if they wouldn't mind.

*Student's thought:*

*"I'm really feeling furious*
*At earnings so penurious.*
*Are sponsors' motives spurious?*
*How come <u>there's no one</u> curious?*
*This whole affair is scurrilous."*

# Justice is Served

*Author's note: This was inspired by an article by Joe Drape: "Penn State to Pay Nearly $60 Million to 26 Abuse Victims", New York Times, October 28, 2013.*

*Preamble:*

*A student in need*
*is pathetic indeed*
*If he <u>has</u> to avoid sex abuse.*
*A Hero with Glory*
*Should be his <u>real</u> story*
*For anything less, no excuse.*


Award for Victims hurt when young
While "legions" closed their eyes,
Including staff and sponsors
Who all "professed" surprise.


Besides the payments there will be
More money for the teams,
While scholarships increased controls
Will actualize their dreams.

# Multi-Media: Marathon Man

A deception has come to the fore
Our marathon Heroes galore.
After years of suspicion and flouted permission
Now confess and admit the real score.

They've been doping and lying for years
We never guessed this was the case.
Our heroes are wilted, our trust has been jilted,
Oh—how can we ever save face?

As we open our minds to the scene
We're aware of a subtle machine.
Corporate powers who feign *"not for profit and gain"*
Are involved and from guilt they abstain.

There are many beyond down the line
Who profess a "blind eye" but abet.
So that athletes then know just how far they can go
Which ensnares them as part of the net.

The denouement has yet to appear,
It's a scandal that won't disappear.
Many questions arise where the truth really lies,
And where do we take it from here?

The answer for this must include
The deceit and destruction accrued—
Not enough just to list what will always be missed:
Defamation of National mood.

We must all work hard to restore,
Our old native Esprit de Corps.
Our pledge is that now as before—
We shall all live with Honor once more.

## Boys Will Be Boys

*Author's note:*
*This was inspired by the Miami Dolphins and the NFL.*

"Boys will be boys"
Doesn't shut out the noise
That the NFL scandal's about

There was
    Sexual,
      Sadistic,
        And racial maligning,
          Familial name-calling,
            And tortured confining.

The men are not boys
    But they
      Acted like kids
        And need time
          In cold storage
            For losing their lids.

# Our Hero–Disrobed: Lance Armstrong[14] and the Tour de France

*Author's note: This was inspired by the* New York Times *article* "Looking Upstream in Doping Cases" *by Claudio Gatti, January 16, 2013, page B11.*

The Lance Armstrong Saga had plenty of style,
He "hooked" all as he passed on his bike.
We admired his smile as he rode mile by mile,
Now we're shouting, "Hey, Lance—Take a hike!"

The story that's just being brought into view
Is familiar, it's shameful, and sad.
We wish he could do what he told us was true—
That might keep us from feeling so bad.

He took drugs and lied (and kept secrets inside),
And the sponsors made money at first.
But then it got risky as "donors" got frisky,
Success <u>didn't</u> quench corporate thirst.

---

[14] "A prominent part of the cycling scene that received less attention, however, was the corporate sponsors that paid handsomely to hitch their brands to a global star.... Companies that endorse athletes might prefer to stand by quietly if they know an athlete is doping, appreciating the benefits of his success rather than moving to expose their pitchman."

The money was flowing and no one was knowing
What actually was the real case.
The thrills kept on coming, which kept the cash humming
Which was a "good" reason to race.

One by one clients shifted and lifted endorsements,
When news about doping came out.
But big corporations and U.S. post, too
Just "assumed" most details were in doubt.

As long as a sponsor was rarely accused
Instructions were "on with the show—"
*"We want you to do what you know you can do
Don't get caught, 'cause I don't want to know."*

When Armstrong was interviewed on Oprah's show,
He confessed the extent of his crime.
But he didn't "connect" it to let himself know
He'd been cheating us all of the time.

It's amazing what we all can hide from ourselves
If we think we are willing to try.
Do we think we'll feel "safer" if we "forget" facts
Because then it's not really a lie?

All involved "played the game" and "pretended" no shame
'Til the anti-dope "Bona Fide" team.
Read the file for awhile, and with grim and stern style,
Woke everyone up from their dream.

1. Ralph D. Russo, "Te'o Messages Played", *New York Times*, January 24, 2013.
2. Top Articles "The five most viewed articles viewed from Jan 11 – 17." *New York Times.*
3. Taylor Branch, "The Shame of College Sports", *Atlantic Magazine*, October 11, 2011.
4. Claudio Gatti, "Looking Upstream in Doping Cases.", *New York Times*, January 15, 2013
5. Tom Archdeacon, "Elite Young Athletes Vulnerable to Sex Abuse." *Dayton Daily News*, July 22, 2012

# Sport Scene in Flux

The sport scene of late is enduring a fate
Which has ramifications galore.
Not just the drugs and the race to the top
The question now growing
Is where will this stop?
Has it been this pervasive before?

Not just on the courts, or the fields or the schools
It's "filtering" into our fans.
They're accepting, expecting, and watch as they grin
"crooked" sports are the current game plan.
Is this what we want our children to learn
That the motive for play is "money to burn"?

# "Hanky Panky"

"Hanky Panky"
Can we afford it?

Our mind's eye portrays our ideal
Towards unblemished honor we feel
Our goals are the purest, our pathway the surest,
Our values boast moral appeal.

How then do we tolerate fraud?
We close our mind's eye and applaud.
We profess to be highest, but actions belie us
Our record for honesty flawed.

## Penetrating the Imponderable: Hoarding and Having

*Author's note: This was inspired by a flurry of articles in the press about hoarding which suggested that the current generation is the most acquisitive.*

*We're moving out onto a brand-new purview*
*And it's strange. I'm not sure where it leads.*
*There's no comfort in it, its change without limit,*
*And I sure hope this new way succeeds.*

There's nothing new when we fear change
We're used to what we know
And each new stage is there to teach
A way we're sure to grow.

I'm sure throughout the Ages
The Sages had their doubt
Giving up or turning back
Reveals exactly what we'd lack
Is buying more what life's about?
CAN'T WE EXIST
AND DO WITHOUT?

# Enough is Enough is Enough–Guns

We're all ready to say "It's Enough!"
And to puncture Society's bluff.
We've been riding so high on the hog,
It's been blinding to see through the fog

But Starbucks is saying "NO MORE"
And forbidding all guns in the store.
It takes some with guts and stern stuff
To repeat and insist, "It's Enough!"

Now it's our time to really get tough
And insist that enough is enough.

# The New Way: The Future

# Kyrielle for the Future

The movies come, the movies go
Each one announced with whoop and holler
As expectations duly grow
We stand in line and pay the dollar

The sales are on and we all run
No matter if we're clerk or scholar
Anticipating prize well won
We stand in line and pay the dollar

How many times on life's long road
We lose the lead and merely "foller"
And, not yet knowing what's bestowed
We stand in line and pay the dollar

# Pantoum[15]

The world is such a mess today
With no one knowing what to do.
If we all try we'll find a way.
Forget the old, begin anew.

With no one knowing what to do
Our life goes on from bad to worse.
Forget the old, begin anew.
We've got to save the universe.

Our life goes on from bad to worse
We really need a working plan.
We've got to save the universe.
Let's start discussions man to man.

We really need a working plan.
At least on this we all agree.
Let's start discussions man to man
And then we'll see what we can see.

---

[15] Pantoum is a fifteenth-century Malaysian short folk poem comprised of two rhymed couplets. Victor Hugo and other Western poets altered this to four stanzas illustrated with a "circular" formal, repetitive rhyme scheme.

"The modern pantoum is a poem of any length, composed of four-line stanzas in which the second and fourth lines of each stanza serve as the first and third lines of the next stanza." See more at: www.poets.org/viewmedia.php/prmMID/5786.

At least on this we all agree
Perhaps it's somewhere to begin
And then we'll see what we can see
Besides the awful mess we're in.

Perhaps it's somewhere to begin
We must do something to survive
Besides the awful mess we're in
The main thing is, keep hope alive.

We must do something to survive.
The world is such a mess today.
The main thing is, keep hope alive.
If we all try we'll find a way.

# Who Knows?

Who knows what the future brings us?
No one has a crystal ball.
One thing we may all depend on . . .
There will be some change for all.
Even as we strive to keep it
(We are used to where we are.)
Time moves on in one direction.
Hitch your wagon to a star.

Better to look up for guidance,
Looking down infers defeat.
Change has always been traumatic
But it's better than retreat.

# Wishful Thinking

*With respectful deference to Joyce Kilmer*

I think that I would like to see
A change on which we'd all agree.

Where many folks can share their views
Or disagree if so they choose.

And this occurs when folks respect
An idea that they did not expect.

But even so, they take it in,
And shrug their shoulders with a grin.

*They'll Say:*

"You've got a right to think your way,
Or roll your eyes at what I say."

Okay to wait 'til facts come in
And <u>then</u> decide just who will win.

A person who can see a trap
And chooses truth instead of pap.

Who picks the leaders who will care
About the needs to make life fair.

Honest statesman's what we need
To stop the cheating, graft, and greed.

The future's made by folks like me.
Let's choose to change so we'll stay free.

Invitation

Just one. Only one.
Close your eyes and visualize . . .

A path that's strewn
with harvested hopes
Of challenges taken and won.

Warm breezes wafting gently
Into the spaces ahead. . . .
A harbinger of happiness.

Oh! Take one. Only one. . . .

Step into tomorrow.

# "Pax Vobiscum"

*(Peace Be Unto You)*

Our hopes today reveal an ancient dream
Which yearns for man to live in harmony and peace
When wars would end and enmity would cease
But nations find this difficult to do
Thus live in fear and hold a jaundiced view
This but postpones the long-held wish for man
To live with love by this Eternal plan

Along the Way

## Rainbow

Red and Yellow, White and Brown
Black and many shades thereof
Rainbow families are our future
In a world we build with love.

In the wide world there are places
Where the "call" has not yet come
We alone move toward our future
As our soul awaits the drum.

# Photo Gallery

"Where are the cows? Tova 'waiting for the cows to come home.' Young Tova (four years old), born in Philadelphia, PA, in 1929."

*"High School Graduation, 1945. Tova, age 16."*

"Getting a Smile out of Harold. Tova and Harold. Taken in 2004 during a family cruise to the Bahamas in honor of her husband's 80th birthday celebration."

"Family photo at Harold Milinsky's 80th birthday party, 2004. Row 1: Harold Finkleman, Jeff Axelrod, Yvonne Milinsky, Travis Wright, Lee Blizman, Assad Sobky. Row 2: Jamie Axelrod, Sara Axelrod, Ariel Dovana Milinsky, Vanessa Henderkien Wright, Alexis Blizman, Paul Blizman. Row 3: Beth Hedva, Joel Milinsky, Tova Milinsky, Harold Milinsky, Debby Milinsky, Sharon Milinsky.

Great Group of Super Ladies

"Tova's Arizona writing group with their teacher, Marilyn McGrath, 2008. Phoebe Maurer, Tova Milinsky, Lois Jamieson, Marilyn McGrath, Mary Wehrenberg, Estelle Lazell, Ann Graf, Krystyna Jasper, Betsy Varcarolis."

# About the Author

*"Tova Milinsky, 2013."*

*Tova Sylvia Snyder Milinsky* knows about "along the way." Born July 2, 1929, to Wolf Vladimer Snyder and Helen Eleanor Greenbaum in Philadelphia, Pennsylvania, at the age of four she moved to New York to live with her Aunt Rose and Uncle Paul Greenbaum, and younger cousin, Sandra. The following year, she moved in with her grandmother, Fanny Gibian Greenbaum, and uncles Willie,

Herbert and partner Carl. Her teen years were spent with her Aunt Dorothy and her husband, Morrie Lovett. After graduating high school at the age of sixteen, she moved to Detroit where she joined her father, Wolf, and his new wife, Esther Slatkin-Ashkenazy Snyder, with her new family, seven-year-old David and new little sister, six-month-old Lee. There, Tova joined a new circle of friends, met and married Dr. Harold C. Milinsky, raised four children, earned a master's degree in social work from Wayne State University in 1966, and worked as a clinical social worker until 1993. She has five grandchildren. Tova currently lives half the year in Scottsdale, Arizona, and half the year in Beverly Hills, Michigan.